Big-Eyed Amphibians

Frogs are amphibians

with big, bulging eyes.

Their big eyes see

in almost all directions.

Table of Contents

Pebble Plus is published by Capstone Press,
151 Good Counsel Drive, P.O. Box 669, Mankato, Minnesota 56002.
www.capstonepress.com

092009
005618CGS10

 Books published by Capstone Press are manufactured with paper
containing at least 10 percent post-consumer waste.

Library of Congress Cataloging-in-Publication Data
Sweeney, Alyse.
  Frogs / by Alyse Sweeney.
   p. cm. — (Pebble plus. Amphibians)
  Includes bibliographical references and index.
  Summary: "Simple text and photographs present frogs, how they look, where they live,
and what they do" — Provided by publisher.
   ISBN 978-1-4296-3987-3 (library binding)
   ISBN 978-1-4296-4849-3 (paperback)
   1. Frogs — Juvenile literature. I. Title.
QL668.E2S938 2010
597.8'9 — dc22   2009024743

Editorial Credits
Jenny Marks, editor; Lori Bye, designer; Marcie Spence, media researcher; Eric Manske, production specialist

All diagram illustrations are by Kristin Kest.

Photo Credits
fotolia/Isabelle Barthe, 11
iStockphoto/fotoIE, 17
Shutterstock/Audrey Snider-Bell, 21; basel101658, 13; Christopher Tan Teck Hean, 7; Eduard Kyslynskyy, 1, 9; Gilles
    DeCruyenaere, 5; Sebastian Duda, cover; Steve Adamson, 15

Note to Parents and Teachers

The Amphibians set supports national science standards related to life science. This book
describes and illustrates frogs. The images support early readers in understanding the text. The
repetition of words and phrases helps early readers learn new words. This book also introduces
early readers to subject-specific vocabulary words, which are defined in the Glossary section.
Early readers may need assistance to read some words and to use the Table of Contents,
Glossary, Read More, Internet Sites, and Index sections of the book.

Amphibians

Frogs

by Alyse Sweeney

Consulting editor: Gail Saunders-Smith, PhD

Consultant: Linda Weir
USGS Patuxent Wildlife Research Center
Laurel, Maryland

WITHDRAWN

CAPSTONE PRESS
a capstone imprint

Frogs are found
on every continent
except Antarctica.
They live on land, in water,
and in trees.

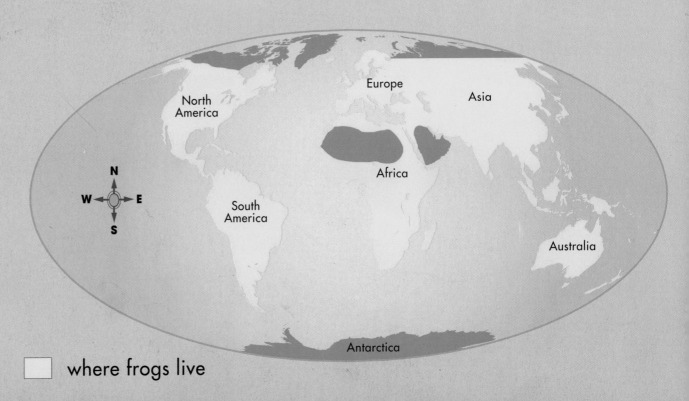

North America

Europe

Asia

Africa

South America

Australia

N
W E
S

Antarctica

□ where frogs live

Frog Bodies

The biggest frogs
grow up to 12 inches
(30 centimeters) long.
The smallest are .6 inch
(1.5 centimeters) long.

Some frogs have long

back legs to swim and leap.

Other frogs have

short, thick back legs

to burrow into the ground.

Green and brown frogs
hide from predators.
They blend in with grass,
plants, mud, and water.

Few predators eat
red, yellow, or blue frogs.
Bright skin colors
are a warning
that a frog tastes bad.

Frog Food

Frogs eat insects, worms,

and other small animals.

Most frogs catch prey

with their long, sticky tongues.

A Frog's Life

As a frog grows,

its body changes

through metamorphosis.

Adult frogs lay eggs in water.

Tadpoles hatch from the eggs.

Frog Life Cycle

egg

tadpole

adult

Tadpoles grow legs
and lungs.
Tails and gills disappear
as the tadpoles
become adult frogs.

Glossary

blend — to fit in with surroundings

bulge — to swell out like a lump

burrow — a tunnel or hole in the ground made or used by an animal

gill — a body part on the side of a tadpole that helps it get oxygen underwater; a tadpole's gills start to close after four weeks.

hatch — to break out of an egg

metamorphosis — the changes that some animals go through as they develop from eggs to adults

predator — an animal that hunts other animals for food

prey — an animal hunted by other animals for food

warning — a sign of possible danger

Read More

Arnosky, Jim. *All About Frogs.* New York: Scholastic, 2008.

Carney, Elizabeth. *Frogs!* National Geographic Kids. Washington, D.C.: National Geographic, 2009.

Milbourne, Anna. *Tadpoles and Frogs.* Usborne Beginners. New York: Random House, 2007.

Internet Sites

FactHound offers a safe, fun way to find Internet sites related to this book. All of the sites on FactHound have been researched by our staff.

Here's all you do:

Visit *www.facthound.com*

FactHound will fetch the best sites for you!

Index

Word Count: 160
Grade: 1
Early-Intervention Level: 17